RACHEL CARSON

Extraordinary Environmentalist

Jill C. Wheeler

ABDO Publishing Company

visit us at
www.abdopublishing.com

Published by ABDO Publishing Company, PO Box 398166, Minneapolis, MN 55439. Copyright © 2013 by Abdo Consulting Group, Inc. International copyrights reserved in all countries. No part of this book may be reproduced in any form without written permission from the publisher. The Checkerboard Library™ is a trademark and logo of ABDO Publishing Company.

Printed in the United States of America, North Mankato, Minnesota.
052012
092012

 PRINTED ON RECYCLED PAPER

Cover Photos: Getty Images; Thinkstock
Interior Photos: Getty Images pp. 5, 17, 23, 25, 27; iStockphoto pp. 7, 25; Pennsylvania College for Women/Chatham College Archives, Chatham University p. 13; used by permission of Rachel Carson Council, Inc. pp. 6, 9, 11, 15; courtesy of US Fish and Wildlife Service pp. 19, 21

Series Coordinator: BreAnn Rumsch
Editors: Megan M. Gunderson, BreAnn Rumsch
Art Direction: Neil Klinepier

Library of Congress Cataloging-in-Publication Data

Wheeler, Jill C., 1964-
  Rachel Carson : extraordinary environmentalist / Jill C. Wheeler.
     p. cm. -- (Women in science)
  Includes index.
  ISBN 978-1-61783-446-2
  1. Carson, Rachel, 1907-1964--Juvenile literature. 2. Biologists--United States--Biography--Juvenile literature. 3. Environmentalists--United States--Biography--Juvenile literature. I. Title.
  QH31.C33W43 2013
  570.92--dc23
  [B]
                              2012004886

CONTENTS

Rachel Carson 4

Allegheny Girl 6

Solitary Student 8

A New Interest 12

Graduate Studies 14

Back to Writing 16

Aquatic Biologist 18

A New Career 20

Dangerous Ground 22

A New Movement 24

A Voice for Nature 26

Timeline 28

Dig Deeper 29

Glossary 30

Web Sites 31

Index 32

RACHEL CARSON

> "The more clearly we can focus our attention on the wonders and realities of the universe about us, the less taste we shall have for destruction."
>
> — *Rachel Carson*

Rachel Carson is known for sparking the modern **environmental** movement. She was an enthusiastic **biologist**. She shared her love of nature and science through her writing.

By the 1950s, Carson had serious concerns about how **pesticides** were being used. Carson's interest in this issue led her to write a book called *Silent Spring*. In it, she argues that all life is connected, from insects to people. She also questions the harmful effects of chemicals on the environment.

Millions of people read Carson's book. They became concerned, too. It even led to government action to protect the environment. The book gave nature a voice.

Carson's influence continued after her death. In 1980, President Jimmy Carter

awarded her the Presidential Medal of Freedom. This is the highest award a civilian can earn. Today, Carson's words continue to inspire people to make better choices for the **environment**.

ALLEGHENY GIRL

Rachel Louise Carson was born on May 27, 1907, in Springdale, Pennsylvania. She was Robert and Maria Carson's third child. Robert worked as a salesman. Maria managed their home and took care of the children.

Rachel's older sister was named Marian, and her older brother was named Robert. Marian and Robert were already in school when Rachel was born.

So, young Rachel spent the days at home with her mother. Maria loved being outside among the many plants and animals. She began to share that love with her daughter when Rachel was barely a year old. The two spent many hours in the woods and fields of the family's 64-acre (26-ha) farm.

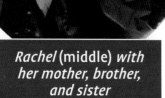

Rachel (middle) *with her mother, brother, and sister*

Rachel also loved to spend time in the woods along the Allegheny River. She often found something exciting to bring home and show her mother. The two would talk about Rachel's latest discovery.

Afterward, Rachel would carefully take the item back to where she had found it. Her mother taught her that doing no harm to nature was part of loving it.

Rachel's interest in the sea blossomed from time spent exploring her family's land. She once found a shell and wondered how it had come to be so far from the ocean.

SOLITARY STUDENT

Rachel grew up attending School Street School. But, she sometimes missed classes. Rachel's family lived far from town. She couldn't go if the weather was bad. Other times, illness among the students kept her home.

Before she married, Rachel's mother had been a teacher. So, Maria taught Rachel at home when she had to miss school. This helped Rachel's grades stay among the highest in her class.

Maria also shared her love of books with her youngest daughter. Even as a child, Rachel wanted to be a writer. When she was eight years old, she began making her own books with illustrations.

In 1918, 11-year-old Rachel wrote a story called "A Battle in the Clouds." She sent it to a magazine called *St. Nicholas*. The magazine held a monthly contest for young writers. Rachel's story won!

Rachel continued to write stories. During this time, Rachel's brother served in **World War I**. He was in the Army Air Service. So, many of Rachel's stories were about war heroes. *St. Nicholas* published four of her stories in one year!

As a child, writing and nature were Rachel's greatest loves.

Rachel's distance from town became more of a problem as she grew older. There was no high school in Springdale. Some families sent their children to schools in other towns. But that meant money for train fare. Rachel's family had no extra money.

Luckily, School Street School offered some classes for ninth and tenth grade students. So, Rachel went there for two more years.

In 1923, Rachel attended high school in Parnassus, a town two miles (3 km) from Springdale. Maria taught piano lessons to help pay for Rachel's transportation to and from school.

At Parnassus High School, Rachel continued to be an outstanding student. She had some trouble making friends. But, she played team sports including field hockey and basketball.

In high school, Rachel was driven to succeed.
She worked hard and always gave her best.

A New Interest

Rachel graduated from high school in May 1925. Maria decided Rachel would attend Pennsylvania College for Women (PCW) in Pittsburgh. Today, the school is known as Chatham University.

To pay for her classes, Rachel's father sold some of their land. Her mother took on more piano students. And, Rachel earned a **scholarship**. She had just enough to make ends meet.

Rachel decided to study English and become a writer. Between classes, she enjoyed playing field hockey. She also liked visiting the Carnegie Museum of Natural History.

Like many girls, Rachel's clothes were homemade. However, she lacked the social skills of many of her classmates. She had no interest in dances, tea parties, or social gatherings.

These things had not been important at home. But they mattered at PCW. So, Rachel never quite fit in with her classmates. Still, she didn't let this affect her goals.

At PCW, Rachel took as many science classes as she could. Her favorite biology professor, Mary Scott Skinker, remained a friend for life.

During her second year at PCW, Rachel's life changed. She decided to take a **biology** class. Rachel realized that science was a perfect fit for her love of nature. So she decided to also study science. She especially wanted to learn about the sea.

GRADUATE STUDIES

During Rachel's final two years at PCW, her interest in science grew. She decided to study **biology** instead of English. Then, she began making plans to study science in graduate school.

In June 1929, Rachel graduated from PCW. She was one of only three students in her class of 70 to graduate with **honors**.

Rachel's good grades earned her an eight-week **fellowship**. It was at Cape Cod's **Marine** Biological Laboratory in Woods Hole, Massachusetts. Rachel also won money to pay for classes at Johns Hopkins University in Baltimore, Maryland. She spent three years studying **zoology** and other sciences there.

In 1931, Rachel changed her focus to marine biology. She graduated in 1932. Yet Rachel wasn't ready to stop learning. So, she entered a **PhD** program at Johns Hopkins.

Meanwhile, Rachel's family was struggling to make ends meet. Rachel invited them to live with her. The move did little to improve the family's finances. So, Rachel took a part-time job teaching at the University of Maryland.

Rachel worked hard to continue her education. But with little time or money, her dream fell out of reach. She dropped out of Johns Hopkins in 1934.

Rachel's love of the sea was fully realized at Woods Hole. Her time there likely inspired her many books about the ocean.

BACK TO WRITING

While Carson taught part-time, she searched for more work. Yet, jobs were hard to find. Then in July 1935, Carson's father died.

Shortly after this, Carson contacted her former **biology** professor Mary Scott Skinker. Skinker was working at the US Department of Agriculture. She suggested that Carson take the federal civil service test. A passing score would qualify her for a government job.

Carson passed the test. In October 1935, the US Bureau of Fisheries in Washington DC hired her. Carson wrote scripts for a radio program on **marine** biology topics.

The radio program had been on the air for some time. Yet, it had failed to reach a wide audience. No one had been able to present scientific information in a way that average people found interesting.

With writing experience and a science background, Carson was perfect for the job. Her supervisor loved her work and asked her to write more.

Carson also sold stories to the *Baltimore Sun* newspaper. Her work helped provide for her family.

Carson's work with the US Bureau of Fisheries was groundbreaking. She was one of just two women not employed as a secretary or in another support role.

Aquatic Biologist

In 1936, the US Bureau of Fisheries hired Carson as a junior **aquatic biologist**. She interviewed fishermen and scientists. She visited laboratories and field stations. She studied Chesapeake Bay's fish and wrote about what she found.

During her free time, Carson continued to write stories about the sea. The *Atlantic Monthly* magazine published her first major story, "Undersea," in 1937. Carson felt more sure about her writing. So she followed the story with her first book. *Under the Sea-Wind* was published in 1941.

Carson also continued to advance in her career. In 1949, she became editor-in-chief for the US Fish and Wildlife Service (FWS). She reviewed brochures and wrote speeches. She also oversaw the organization's library and staff.

Carson was busy and successful. But, it was the sea that she truly loved to write about. So Carson soon began to work on another book.

The Rachel Carson National Wildlife Refuge in Maine was named in her honor in 1969.

CONSERVATION IN ACTION

Number ONE
Fish and Wildlife

CHINCOTEAGUE
a National Wildlife Refuge

Service, United States Department of the Interior, Washington, D. C.

One of Carson's FWS brochures

A New Career

Carson spent two years researching her next book. *The Sea Around Us* was published in 1951. Critics and readers loved it.

The book spent 86 weeks on the *New York Times* best-seller list. It won the National Book Award in 1952. And, the book was printed in 32 languages. It was even made into a documentary film that won an Academy Award.

The success of *The Sea Around Us* changed Carson's life. By 1952, she was able to quit her job and write full time. She was also able to care for her mother and other family members.

Writing was the perfect job for Carson. In 1955, she published *The Edge of the Sea*. It spent 20 weeks on the *New York Times* best-seller list. For her success, Carson was elected to the American Academy of Arts and Letters. But her greatest success was still to come.

During the early 1950s, Carson took several trips to Florida. There, she explored seashore life for her book The Edge of the Sea.

DANGEROUS GROUND

>> *DDT was first used to fight insects during World War II. Later, it was used on US farmland.*

By the 1950s, Carson had become interested in a new subject area. Few studies had been done on the long-term effects of **pesticides** on the **environment**. Carson was concerned about the plants, animals, and people exposed to chemicals such as DDT. She began to research the issue.

Carson talked to people who had seen DDT in action. Some had seen insects become resistant after repeated exposure. Others had seen desirable insects and birds killed off.

Carson learned the chemicals stayed in the ground and in water. She also found evidence that they stayed in people's bodies. Some researchers even believed the chemicals caused **cancer**.

Carson's alarm convinced her to draw attention to these dangers. She developed a large network of scientists, naturalists, journalists, and activists. She listened to their ideas and took many notes.

In 1963, Carson talked about her research for Silent Spring *on television.*

Carson also contacted federal officials for information. And, she studied court cases on the topic. After four years of careful research, Carson had a solid story.

The New Yorker magazine published "Silent Spring" in June 1962 in three parts. Carson also turned the story into a book. It was published that September.

A New Movement

Silent Spring details how **pesticides** do more harm than good. At the time, the air, water, and ground were becoming polluted. And insects were growing resistant to pesticides.

Birds exposed to DDT developed problems laying healthy eggs. Fewer birds meant less birdsong in the springtime. This would lead to a silent spring.

Right away, Carson came under fire for the book's message. But the book did not say that pesticides should be banned. Rather, it argued that more research was needed to learn how these chemicals affect living things.

Still, the chemical industry called Carson an **alarmist**. Some people accused her of trying to harm American food production.

Carson understood these reactions. Powerful companies sold more than $1 billion worth of the products each year. But Carson was prepared to defend her work.

Pesticides are often sprayed on crop fields (below). But they affect more than just pests. For example, DDT caused many birds to lay eggs with weak shells (right).

A VOICE FOR NATURE

>> In 1970, President Richard Nixon created the Environmental Protection Agency (EPA). DDT use in the United States was banned in 1972.

Silent Spring quickly captured the nation's attention. The federal government ordered a review of its policy on **pesticide** use. In 1963, Carson spoke before members of Congress. They determined Carson's facts were indeed correct.

Silent Spring caused people to demand that the government protect the **environment**. President John F. Kennedy ordered safety testing of pesticides. As soon as 1963, many state legislatures introduced bills to limit pesticide use.

Carson had won the battle to get people to think about protecting the environment. However, she had a personal battle to fight as well. While writing *Silent Spring*, she had been diagnosed with **cancer**. Carson died on April 14, 1964, at her home in Silver Spring, Maryland.

During her 56 years, Rachel Carson turned her love of nature into a successful career. Her words offered people a new view of the world. And, her scientific skills gave them reason to trust her. Thanks to Carson, nature's beauty can be enjoyed for generations to come.

The Sense of Wonder *was published after Carson's death. The book aims to plant a love of nature in children.*

TIMELINE

1907
On May 27, Rachel Louise Carson was born in Springdale, Pennsylvania.

1918
Rachel began her writing career at age 11, with the publication of her first short story.

1929
Rachel graduated from Pennsylvania College for Women in Pittsburgh, Pennsylvania.

1932
Rachel graduated from Johns Hopkins University in Baltimore, Maryland.

1935
Carson began writing for a US Bureau of Fisheries radio program.

1941
Carson's first book, *Under the Sea-Wind*, was published.

1949
Carson was named editor-in-chief of the US Fish and Wildlife Service.

1951
Carson published *The Sea Around Us*.

1955
The Edge of the Sea was published.

1962
Carson's book *Silent Spring* angered the chemical industry and started the environmental movement.

1963
Carson spoke about pesticide use with members of Congress.

1964
Carson died on April 14, after battling with cancer.

DIG DEEPER

As a biologist, Rachel Carson understood that all living things are connected. Explore this idea further by building your own terrarium!

SUPPLIES:
- 2 clear, clean 2-liter soda bottles without labels • a marker • X-ACTO knife
- a ruler • 6 inches (15 cm) of cotton string • potting soil • plant seeds • water

INSTRUCTIONS: *Always ask an adult for help!*

1. Measure 5 inches (13 cm) down from the top of one bottle and 4 inches (10 cm) up from the bottom of the other. Draw lines around the bottles at these points. Ask an adult to use the knife to cut the bottles in half along the lines. Keep both top sections and the short bottom section.

2. Ask an adult to use the tip of the knife to cut a hole in one of the bottle caps. The hole should be large enough for the string to pass through. Soak the string in water and thread it through the hole. Twist the cap onto the tall top section. About 1 inch (2.5 cm) of string should hang outside the top of the cap.

3. Turn the tall top section upside down and fill it with five inches (13 cm) of potting soil. Make sure the string runs up from the cap through the soil to the soil's surface.

4. Add water to the short bottom section. Place the soil-filled top section in it with the bottle cap down. The string should be in the water.

5. Plant your seeds in the soil and water according to the directions on the seed packet. Cover with the short top section, twist on the second bottle cap, and place your terrarium in a sunny place.

Watch your terrarium for the next few days and weeks. How long did it take for your plants to begin growing? What elements are in the bottle that allow the plants to live? What do you think would happen if a new plant was added to the bottle? An insect? A chemical?

GLOSSARY

alarmist – a person who spreads unreasonable fear about something.

aquatic – growing or living in water.

biology – the study of living things, especially plants and animals. A scientist who studies biology is a biologist.

cancer – any of a group of often deadly diseases marked by harmful changes in the normal growth of cells. Cancer can spread and destroy healthy tissues and organs.

environment – all the surroundings that affect the growth and well-being of a living thing.

fellowship – the position of a person appointed for advanced study or research.

honors – special attention given to a graduating student for high academic achievement.

marine – of or relating to the sea.

pesticide (PEHS-tuh-side) – a substance used to destroy pests.

PhD – doctor of philosophy. Usually, this is the highest degree a student can earn.

scholarship - money or aid given to help a student continue his or her studies.

World War I - from 1914 to 1918, fought in Europe. Great Britain, France, Russia, the United States, and their allies were on one side. Germany, Austria-Hungary, and their allies were on the other side.

zoology - a branch of biology that deals with animals and their behavior.

WEB SITES

To learn more about Rachel Carson, visit ABDO Publishing Company online. Web sites about Rachel Carson are featured on our Book Links page. These links are routinely monitored and updated to provide the most current information available.

www.abdopublishing.com

INDEX

A
Allegheny River 7
American Academy of
    Arts and Letters 20

B
"Battle in the Clouds,
    A" 8
biology 4, 13, 14, 16, 18
birth 6
Bureau of Fisheries, US
    16, 17, 18

C
Carter, Jimmy 4, 5
Chesapeake Bay 18
childhood 6, 7, 8, 10

D
DDT 22, 24
death 4, 26

E
Edge of the Sea, The 20
education 8, 10, 12, 13,
    14, 15
environmental movement
    4, 5, 26

F
family 6, 7, 8, 10, 12,
    14, 15, 16, 17, 20
Fish and Wildlife
    Service, US 18

H
hobbies 6, 7, 8, 10, 12

K
Kennedy, John F. 26

M
Marine Biological
    Laboratory 14
marine biology 14, 16
Maryland 14, 15, 26
Massachusetts 14

N
National Book Award 20

P
Pennsylvania 6, 7, 10, 12
pesticides 4, 22, 24, 26
Presidential Medal of
    Freedom 5

S
Sea Around Us, The 20
"Silent Spring" (article)
    23
Silent Spring (book) 4,
    23, 24, 26
Skinker, Mary Scott 16

U
Under the Sea-Wind 18
"Undersea" 18

W
Washington DC 16

Z
zoology 14